The Adventures of Tom Sawyer

MARK TWAIN

Level 1

Retold by Jacqueline Kehl
Series Editors: Andy Hopkins and Jocelyn Potter

Pearson Education Limited
Edinburgh Gate, Harlow,
Essex CM20 2JE, England
and Associated Companies throughout the world.

ISBN: 978-1-4058-4277-8

First published 1876
Published by Puffin Books 1950
First published by Penguin Books 2000
This edition published 2008

17

Text copyright © Penguin Books 2000
This edition copyright © Pearson Education Ltd 2008

Typeset by Graphicraft Ltd, Hong Kong
Set in 12/14pt Bembo
Printed in China
SWTC/17

Published by Pearson Education Ltd

Acknowledgements

Every effort has been made to trace the copyright holders and we apologise
in advance for any unintentional omissions. We would be pleased to insert the
appropriate acknowledgement in any subsequent edition of this publication.

For a complete list of the titles available in the Pearson English Readers series, please
visit www.pearsonenglishreaders.com. Alternatively, write to your local Pearson Education
office or to Pearson English Readers Marketing Department, Pearson Education,
Edinburgh Gate, Harlow, Essex CM20 2JE, England.

Introduction

One Saturday afternoon Tom wanted to have an adventure because he didn't want to think about Injun Joe. He went to Huck and said, "I'm going to look for treasure. Do you want to come with me?"

Tom Sawyer loves adventures. He has a lot of adventures at home, at school, and with his friends. He has one adventure in a cave. But why is he there? What does he see in the cave? And why is he afraid?

Mark Twain (1835–1910) is a famous American writer. His name was Samuel Clemens. Young Samuel lived in Hannibal, Missouri, a small town on the Mississippi River. He loved the river and he liked watching the big boats on it.

Samuel loved adventures. He worked on boats on the Mississippi River for two years. Then he went to Nevada. He looked for treasure, but he didn't find it. He worked for a newspaper there. His stories were in the name of Mark Twain, and people loved them.

Later, Samuel lived in New York. His book *The Adventures of Tom Sawyer* (1876) is about a young boy in a small town in the 1800s. Huck Finn is his friend. *The Adventures of Huckleberry Finn* (1884) is about Huck's adventures. These two books are very famous.

Today, many people visit Hannibal because they want to see Mark Twain's home and the Mark Twain Cave, the cave in *The Adventures of Tom Sawyer*.

Ben started to paint the fence.

Chapter 1   The Fence

Tom Sawyer lived with his aunt because his mother and father were dead. Tom didn't like going to school, and he didn't like working. He liked playing and having adventures. One Friday, he didn't go to school—he went to the river.

Aunt Polly was angry. "You're a bad boy!" she said. "Tomorrow you can't play with your friends because you didn't go to school today. Tomorrow you're going to work for me. You can paint the fence."

Saturday morning, Tom was not happy, but he started to paint the fence. His friend Jim was in the street.

Tom asked him, "Do you want to paint?"

Jim said, "No, I can't. I'm going to get water."

Then Ben came to Tom's house. He watched Tom and said, "I'm going to swim today. You can't swim because you're working."

Tom said, "This isn't work. I like painting."

"Can I paint, too?" Ben asked.

"No, you can't," Tom answered. "Aunt Polly asked me because I'm a very good painter."

Ben said, "I'm a good painter, too. Please, can I paint? I have some fruit. Do you want it?"

"OK," Tom said. "Give me the fruit. Then you can paint."

Ben started to paint the fence. Later, many boys came to Tom's house. They watched Ben, and they wanted to paint, too.

Tom said, "Give me some food and you can paint."

Tom stayed in the yard, and the boys painted. They painted the fence three times. It was beautiful and white.

Tom went into the house. "Aunt Polly, can I play now?" he asked.

Aunt Polly was surprised. "Did you paint the fence?" she asked.

"Yes, I did," Tom answered.

Aunt Polly went to the yard and looked at the fence. She was very surprised and very happy. "It's beautiful!" she said. "Yes, you can play now."

Tom walked to his friend Joe Harper's house and played with his friends there. Then he walked home again. There was a new girl in one yard. She had yellow hair and blue eyes. She was beautiful. Tom wanted to talk to her, but she didn't see him. She went into her house. Tom waited, but she didn't come out again.

Chapter 2   In the Graveyard

One morning before school, Tom's friend Huck Finn waited for him in the street. Huck didn't have a home, and he never went to school. People in the town didn't like him. But Tom liked Huck.

Huck said, "Let's have an adventure."

"What can we do on our adventure?" Tom asked.

"Let's go to the graveyard at night—at twelve o'clock!" Huck answered.

"That's a good adventure," Tom said. "Let's meet at eleven o'clock."

Then Tom went to school, but he was late. The teacher was angry. He asked, "Why are you late again?"

"I'm late because I talked to Huck Finn," Tom said.

Then the teacher was very angry. "Sit with the girls," he said to Tom.

Tom sat near the beautiful new girl. He was happy. He looked at her.

"What's your name?" he asked.

"Becky," she answered.

Tom smiled and said, "My name's Tom."

The teacher was angry again. "Tom Sawyer, stop talking! Go to your place now," he said. Tom went to his place.

At twelve o'clock Tom and Becky didn't go home. They stayed in the school yard and talked. Tom said, "I love you. Do you love me?"

"Yes," Becky answered.

"Good," Tom said. "Then you're going to walk to school with me every day. Amy always walked with me."

"Amy!" Becky said angrily. "Do you love her?"

"No," Tom answered. "I love you now. Do you want to walk with me?"

But Becky was angry with Tom. She walked away and didn't answer. Tom was unhappy. He didn't go to school in the afternoon.

That night Tom went to bed at nine o'clock, but he didn't sleep. At eleven o'clock he went out his bedroom window to the yard. Huck was there. They walked to the graveyard. They stopped behind some big trees and talked quietly.

Suddenly, there was a noise. Three men came into the graveyard—the doctor, Muff Potter, and Injun Joe. Injun Joe and the doctor talked angrily. Then Injun Joe

Then Injun Joe killed the doctor with a knife.

killed the doctor with a knife. Tom and Huck watched. Then they went away quickly because they were afraid.

They went to Tom's yard. Huck said, "We can't talk about this. Injun Joe can find us and kill us, too."

"That's right," Tom said. "We can't talk about it."

Tom went in his bedroom window. He went to bed, but he didn't sleep well. Tom and Huck didn't talk to their friends or Aunt Polly about that night because they were afraid of Injun Joe.

Later, some men went to Muff Potter and said, "You're a bad man. You killed the doctor."

Chapter 3   A Bad Day

Becky was sick and didn't go to school for many days. Tom was very sad. One morning, he said to Aunt Polly, "I'm very sick, and I want to stay home from school."

Aunt Polly said, "Here's some medicine. Take this and you can get well quickly."

But Tom didn't like the medicine. Peter, the cat, came into the room and looked at Tom.

"Peter!" Tom said. "Have some medicine!"

Peter had some medicine. He didn't like it! He went quickly out the open window and into the yard.

Aunt Polly watched Peter. "Why did you do that, Tom?" she asked angrily. "You're a very bad boy! Go to school now."

Tom arrived at school early and he waited for Becky at the school fence. She arrived early, too, but she didn't look at Tom. She went into school. Tom walked away. He didn't want to go to school now. He was very sad.

Joe Harper was near the school. He was sad, too, because his mother was angry with him. The two boys walked and talked.

Tom said, "Let's run away."

"Yes, let's!" Joe said.

The two boys went to the river. Huck Finn was there. Tom and Joe said, "We're going to run away. Do you want to come with us?"

"Yes," Huck answered. "Let's go across the river. We can have a good adventure there."

The boys went home because they wanted to get food for their adventure.

Chapter 4   Across the River

Tom, Joe, and Huck went to the river. There was a small boat there. The boys went across the river in the small boat. They said, "This is a good place because we can play all day. There's no school here."

They played and then went to sleep.

In the morning, the boys were happy again. They said, "Let's stay here for a long time."

In the afternoon, they played near the river again. Suddenly, there was a noise from a big boat on the river. The boys stopped playing and watched the boat.

"Listen," Tom said. "The men on the boat are talking about us."

The boys stopped playing and watched the boat.

The boys listened quietly. A man said, "The boys are in the river. They're dead."

Tom said, "Those men are looking for us in the river. We're here, but they don't know that."

That night, the boys were sad. Huck and Joe went to sleep, but Tom didn't sleep. He went home in the small boat. He quietly went in his bedroom window. Then he went under his bed and stayed there.

Aunt Polly and her friends came into his room. Aunt Polly said to her friends, "Tom was a good boy, and I loved him. Now he's dead, and I'm very sad."

Tom wanted to say, "I'm not dead." But he stayed quiet.

Aunt Polly went to sleep. Tom went out the window very quietly and went back across the river.

In the morning, Joe and Huck said, "We're not happy here now. We want to go home."

Tom said, "Let's go home on Sunday. We can go to church. People are going to be very surprised!"

Sunday morning, many children were at church. They talked about the three boys. They were sad because their friends were dead. Becky was sad, too.

Suddenly, the three boys walked into the church. People were very surprised, but they were very happy, too.

Chapter 5   At School

Monday morning, Tom went to school. The children wanted to hear about his adventure, and Tom liked talking about it. Becky wanted to talk to Tom, but he didn't look at her.

Then Tom talked to Amy. Becky watched him and she was angry. She said to her friends, "I'm going to have an adventure day. You can come on my adventure." But she didn't ask Tom.

Later in the morning, Tom talked to Amy again. Becky talked to her friend Alfred and looked at a picture-book with him. Tom watched them and he was angry with Becky.

In the afternoon, Tom waited for Becky at the school fence. He said, "I'm sorry."

But Becky didn't listen to him. She walked into the school room. The teacher's new book was on his table. This book wasn't for children, but Becky wanted to look at it. She opened the book quietly and looked at the pictures.

Suddenly, Tom came into the room. Becky was surprised. She closed the book quickly, and it tore. Becky was angry with Tom and quickly went out of the room.

Then the children and the teacher came into the room and went to their places. The teacher looked at his book.

"Who did this? Who tore my book?" he asked angrily.

The room was very quiet. The teacher started to ask every child, "Did you do this?"

They answered, "No, I didn't."

Then he looked at Becky. "Becky, did you do this?"

"I did it. I tore your book."

Tom wanted to help her. Suddenly he said, "I did it. I tore your book."

"Tom Sawyer, you're a very bad boy. Stay here after school!" the teacher said angrily.

At five o'clock Tom started to walk home. Becky waited for him at the school fence. "You're a very good friend," she said.

Tom smiled at her and they walked home.

Chapter 6   The Trial

Summer vacation started, and Becky went away with her family. Tom was unhappy.

Then Muff Potter's trial started. Tom and Huck remembered the night in the graveyard. They were afraid of Injun Joe again.

"Did you talk about the night in the graveyard?" Tom asked Huck.

"No, I didn't," Huck answered. "Did you?"

"No," Tom answered. "But I'm sorry about Muff Potter. He's always friendly to us. He didn't kill the doctor. I want to help him."

"Let's take some food to him," Huck said.

The boys visited Muff Potter. "Here's some food," they said.

Muff Potter said, "Thank you. You're good boys."

Tom and Huck went to the trial and listened for two days. Tom didn't sleep well at night because he wanted to help Muff Potter.

On day three of the trial Tom talked.

A man asked him, "Where were you on the night of June 17th?"

"I was in the graveyard," Tom answered.

"Did you see any people there?" the man asked.

"Yes. Injun Joe, the doctor, and Muff Potter were there. They didn't see me because I was behind some big trees."

"What did you see?" the man asked.

"Injun Joe and the doctor talked angrily," Tom answered. "Then Injun Joe killed the doctor with his knife. Muff Potter didn't do it."

The people at the trial were surprised. Injun Joe quickly went out of the building.

Tom and Huck were very afraid. Tom said, "Now Injun Joe knows about us. He can kill *us*, too."

Many people wanted to hear about the boys' adventure in the graveyard. Tom liked talking about it. He was happy, too, because he helped Muff Potter. But he didn't sleep well because he was afraid of Injun Joe.

Chapter 7   Injun Joe's Treasure

One Saturday afternoon, Tom wanted to have an adventure because he didn't want to think about Injun Joe. He went to Huck and said, "I'm going to look for treasure. Do you want to come with me?"

Huck always liked an adventure. "Oh, yes," he said. "Where can we look?"

"Let's start looking in the old house near Mrs. Douglas's house. Old houses are good places for treasure," Tom answered.

The boys went to the old house. They wanted to look at every room. First they went into the kitchen, and then they went into the bedroom.

Suddenly, two men came into the kitchen—Injun Joe and his friend. The boys were afraid and stayed in the bedroom very quietly.

Injun Joe walked across the kitchen. "We can put our money here," he said to his friend.

He started to dig under the floor with his knife.

"What's this?" Injun Joe said. "I'm going to get it out."

There was a big box under the floor. He opened it with his knife. There was a lot of money in the box.

"Look at that money!" his friend said. "Let's go now. We can come back and get it tomorrow."

"No," Injun Joe said. "We're going to take it with us now. We can take it to that place. You know—the place under the cross."

Then the men went out of the house. Injun Joe talked quietly to his friend. The boys listened and were afraid.

Tom said, "Did you hear that? He wants to kill us."

They went out of the house quietly and went home.

The boys were afraid of Injun Joe, but they wanted to find his treasure. They watched his house every night, but they didn't see Injun Joe or his treasure.

There was a lot of money in the box.

Chapter 8   Becky's Adventure Day

In August Becky's family came back from their vacation. Tom was very happy and he didn't think about Injun Joe's treasure.

Becky's adventure day was Saturday. Her mother said, "You can sleep at Susy Harper's house after your adventure."

"Good," Becky said.

Becky and her friends went on the river on a big boat. The boat went down the river and across it. Then it stopped. The children went out of the boat and played games near the river. In the afternoon one boy asked, "Who wants to go to the big cave?"

The children went to the cave. It was dark and cold there, but they played games. In the evening they went back to the boat and went home.

Sunday morning, Becky's mother and Aunt Polly talked to Mrs. Harper at church. Becky's mother asked, "Where's my Becky? Did she sleep at your house?"

"No, she didn't," Mrs. Harper answered. "I didn't see her."

Aunt Polly said, "My Tom didn't come home. Did he stay at your house?"

"No, he didn't," Mrs. Harper answered.

Then Aunt Polly and Becky's mother asked the children, "Did Tom and Becky come home? Did you see them on the boat?"

The children answered, "No, we didn't see them, but it was dark."

Then a boy said, "Maybe they're in the cave!"

Two hundred men looked for Tom and Becky in the cave. They looked for three days, but they didn't find them. People in the town were very sad.

Chapter 9 Huck's Adventure

Huck didn't go on Becky's adventure. He stayed home and watched Injun Joe's house that night. At eleven o'clock Injun Joe and his friend came out and walked down the street. There was a box in his friend's hands.

Huck said quietly, "Maybe that's the treasure box." He went after the two men.

They walked to Mrs. Douglas's house and stopped in her yard. Huck stayed behind some small trees. The men talked, and Huck listened to them.

Injun Joe was angry. "I want to kill her," he said to his friend. "Mr. Douglas was bad to me. He's dead now, but I remember."

"There are a lot of lights in the house. Maybe her friends are visiting," Injun Joe's friend said. "We can come back tomorrow."

"No," Injun Joe said. "Let's wait now."

Huck liked Mrs. Douglas because she was always good to him. He wanted to help her. He quietly walked away and then he started to run to Mr. Jones's house.

Mr. Jones opened the door. "What do you want?" he asked Huck.

"Injun Joe and his friend are in Mrs. Douglas's yard," Huck said. "They want to kill her. Can you go there and help Mrs. Douglas?"

The men talked, and Huck listened to them.

"Yes. My sons and I can go there," Mr. Jones answered. "You can go home."

In the morning, Huck went back to Mr. Jones's house.

"How's Mrs. Douglas?" he asked.

"She's OK," Mr. Jones answered. "The men went away because we arrived."

"Good," Huck said. But he was afraid of Injun Joe. "Please don't say my name to Mrs. Douglas."

Mr. Jones looked at him, and then he said, "You aren't well. Go and sleep in my bedroom."

Later, Mrs. Douglas visited Mr. Jones.

"You helped me yesterday night. Thank you," she said. "You're a good man."

Mr. Jones said, "We didn't know about the men in your yard. A boy was there and he wanted to help you. He came here, but I can't say his name."

Mr. Jones and Mrs. Douglas went to church. People there talked about Tom and Becky. Mr. Jones and his sons went to the cave with the men, but on Monday morning they went home. Huck was in bed and was very sick. The men went back to the cave, but Mrs. Douglas stayed with Huck.

Chapter 10   In the Cave

Saturday, Tom and Becky walked and played in the cave. Then they stopped near some water.

"What time is it?" Becky asked.

"I don't know," Tom said. "Let's go back now."

The two children walked and walked. But they didn't find the door to the cave. Becky was afraid. She wanted to sit down and eat. "Maybe they're looking for us now," she said.

"Here's some food," Tom said. "Eat this and wait here. I'm going to look for the door."

Tom walked and walked. But he didn't find the cave door. Suddenly, there was a man near him. Tom was afraid, but he stayed quiet. He looked at the man. It was Injun Joe!

Tom was very afraid and he made a noise. Injun Joe went away quickly. Tom went back to Becky, but he didn't talk to her about Injun Joe.

They were in the cave for three days. Tuesday, Becky didn't want to walk. Again Tom said, "Stay here. I'm going to look for the door."

This time he went to a new place. There was light there. He went to the light. It came from a small door in the cave.

Tom went out of the cave. Then he went back to Becky. "Come with me," he said. "We can go out of the cave now."

Tom and Becky went out of the cave. They were very happy. They went to the river and waited there. Some men in a small boat came to them.

Tom said, "We want to go home. Can you help us?"

The men answered, "Yes. We can take you home."

Tom and Becky went in the boat with the men. They arrived home very late Tuesday night, and people in the town were very happy. Tom talked all night about their adventure in the cave.

Tom went out of the cave.

Chapter 11   In the Cave Again

Tom and Becky stayed home for many days. Then, two weeks after their adventure, Tom visited Becky and talked to her father.

Mr. Thatcher said, "You're a very good boy, Tom. You helped Becky in the cave. Thank you. People can't go into it now because it has a new big door."

"But Injun Joe's living in the cave!" Tom said.

Some men went down the river to the cave. Tom went with them. They opened the new door. Injun Joe was there, but he was dead.

Tom wanted to talk to Huck. Later in the week he went to Mr. Jones's house. The two boys talked about their adventures.

"The money isn't in Injun Joe's house," Tom said. "It's in the cave! I know, because Injun Joe was there. Let's get it!"

Huck was afraid. "But maybe we can't find it."

"I can find it again," Tom said. "I know about a small door at the back of the cave. Becky and I came out there. We can go in that door, and I can find Injun Joe's treasure."

"OK," Huck said. "Let's go today."

That afternoon the boys went in a small boat to the back of the cave. Tom walked first, and Huck went after him. They walked and walked.

Then Tom said, "This is the right place! Injun Joe was here."

The boys looked for a good place for treasure.

Suddenly, Tom said, "Look! There's a cross! Injun Joe said, 'under the cross.' Let's look there!"

"Look! It's the treasure box!"

The boys went to the place with the cross. Tom said, "I'm going to dig here with my knife . . . Look! It's the treasure box! Let's get it out now. The treasure's ours!"

"This box is very heavy," Huck said. "We can't take it with us."

"I have some small bags," Tom said. "We can put the money in them and take it home."

The boys went out of the cave with the money.

Chapter 12   At Mrs. Douglas's House

Tom said, "Let's take the money to the old house near Mrs. Douglas's house. That's a good place for it."

They started to walk to the old house. Mr. Jones was in Mrs. Douglas's yard. He called to the boys.

"A lot of people are waiting for you. Come with me," he said. They went into Mrs. Douglas's house.

"Hello, boys," Mrs. Douglas said. "Come with me."

Tom and Huck went with her to a bedroom. There were new shirts and jeans on the bed.

"Wash your hands and faces and put on these shirts and jeans," Mrs. Douglas said. "Then come to the big room."

The boys went to the room. A lot of people were there.

Mrs. Douglas said, "First I want to say 'thank you' to Mr. Jones and his sons. They helped me. They're very good people."

"Huck helped, too," Mr. Jones said.

"Thank you, too, Huck," Mrs. Douglas said. "You're a good boy, and I like you. I want to give you a home and some money."

"But Huck has a lot of money!" Tom said.

He went to the bedroom and came back with the bags of money. "We have this money from the cave. There's a lot of money in them, and it's ours now."

There was $12,000 in the bags. The people were very surprised. They asked about the boys' adventure.

Chapter 13 Huck's New Home

Huck lived in the big house with Mrs. Douglas. He was a new person. He washed every day, and he went to school and church. But he wasn't happy. He stayed there for three weeks, and then he ran away.

Tom went to Huck. "Why did you run away?"

Huck answered, "Mrs. Douglas is a good woman. I like her, but I can't live with her. I don't like washing every day, and I don't like going to school and church. I don't want to have a lot of money. But I want to be your friend. OK?"

"No," Tom said, "I can't be your friend, because the boys at school don't want to play with you. We're thinking about a lot of new adventures. Please live with Mrs. Douglas and come to school. Then the boys at school can play with you."

"I want to be your friend," Huck said, "and I want to have adventures with you and the boys at school. Maybe I can live with Mrs. Douglas. I don't know, but I'm going to try it again for a month."

"Good," Tom said. "The boys are meeting later, at twelve o'clock at night. You can come, too."

"Good!" Huck said.

ACTIVITIES

Chapters 1–3

Before you read

1 Read the Introduction. Where did Mark Twain live? What are the names of two of his famous books?

2 Look at the picture of Tom Sawyer and talk about him.
   Is he young or old, fat or thin, happy or sad, tall or short, smart or not very smart, sick or well? What do you think?

3 Do you have adventures? Talk to a friend about one of them.

4 Look at the Word List at the back of the book.
   a Where can Tom visit? Find the words for three places.
   b What can Tom do? Find words for four things.

While you read

5 Who:
   a does Tom Sawyer live with?   ....
   b paint Aunt Polly's fence?   ....
   c doesn't have a home?   ....
   d is angry in the school?   ....
   e is the new girl at school?   ....
   f are in the graveyard at night?   ....
                                               ....
                                               ....
                                               ....
                                               ....
   g kills the doctor?   ....
   h doesn't go to school for many days? ....
   i gives medicine to the cat?   ....
   j want to run away?   ....
                                               ....
                                               ....

25

After you read

6 Are these sentences right or wrong?

    a Tom is a very good student.

    b Tom's friends want to paint Aunt Polly's fence.

    c Aunt Polly is happy with her white fence.

    d Tom is late for school because he went to the graveyard.

    e Tom wants to walk to school with Amy.

    f Tom goes to school every morning and every afternoon.

    g Tom and Huck are afraid of Injun Joe.

    h People in the town say, "Muff Potter killed the doctor."

    i Tom gives medicine to Peter because the cat is sick.

    j Joe Harper has a problem with his mother.

Chapters 4–8

Before you read

7 What do you think?

    a Is Tom Sawyer a bad boy? Why (not)?

    b Is Huck Finn a bad boy? Why (not)?

While you read

8 Put words on the right with words on the left.

    a boats   tore

    b church   dark

    c book   river

    d trial   box

    e money   Muff Potter

    f cave   Sunday

After you read

9 Find the right answer.

    a In their adventure near the river, Tom, Joe, and Huck like to *play/work*.

    b On Sunday morning, people are *happy/sad* because the three boys walk into the church.

c *Amy/Alfred* is Becky's friend at school.

d *Becky/Tom* tore the teacher's book.

e Before the trial, Tom and Huck *talk/don't talk* to their friends about the night in the graveyard.

f At the trial, Tom helps *Muff Potter/Injun Joe*.

g Tom cannot sleep because he is afraid of *Muff Potter/ Injun Joe*.

h Injun Joe and his friend find *a lot of/a little* money in the old house.

i Injun Joe and his friend put the treasure box *under the cross/ in Mrs. Douglas's house*.

j Becky's family *go on/come back from* vacation in August.

k Becky and Tom sleep *in the cave/at Mrs. Harper's house*.

Chapters 9–13

Before you read

10 Talk about these questions. What do you think?

    a What is Injun Joe going to do to Tom and Huck?

    b Are Tom and Becky going to come home?

    c Who is going to have the box of money?

While you read

11 Where are they at this time?

    a Huck finds people. They can help
       Mrs. Douglas. ....

    b Huck is very sick. ....

    c Becky and Tom are afraid. ....

    d Tom talks about his adventures
       in the cave. ....

    e Injun Joe is dead. ....

    f Tom and Huck find Injun Joe's
       treasure. ....

    g Huck gets a new home. ....

After you read

12 Answer the questions.

  a Why does Injun Joe want to kill Mrs. Douglas?

  b Who helps Mrs. Douglas?

  c Why does Huck get sick?

  d Why are Becky and Tom afraid in the cave?

  e Who is Mr. Thatcher? Why does he like Tom?

  f Why is Injun Joe dead?

  g How do Tom and Huck find Injun Joe's treasure box?

  h How does Mrs. Douglas help Huck?

  i Is Huck happy in his new home?

Writing

13 You are Aunt Polly. Sometimes you are angry with Tom, but you love him. Write a letter to your sister about him.

14 You work for the town's newspaper. Write the story: "Town's Doctor Is Dead!"

15 You are Tom's teacher. Write about your problems with him.

16 You are Tom or Huck. What are you going to do with your money from the treasure box? Write about it.

17 Huck is living at Mrs. Douglas's house now. Write about his first three weeks there.

18 You are Tom Sawyer, and you are now a famous man. Write about one of the adventures in this book.